Discovering Mission San Francisco de Asís

BY OSCAR CANTILLO

Cavendish Square
New York

Published in 2016 by Cavendish Square Publishing, LLC
243 5th Avenue, Suite 136, New York, NY 10016

Copyright © 2016 by Cavendish Square Publishing, LLC

First Edition

Website: cavendishsq.com

This publication represents the opinions and views of the author based on his or her personal experience, knowledge, and research. The information in this book serves as a general guide only. The author and publisher have used their best efforts in preparing this book and disclaim liability rising directly or indirectly from the use and application of this book.

CPSIA Compliance Information: Batch #CW16CSQ

All websites were available and accurate when this book was sent to press.

Library of Congress Cataloging-in-Publication Data

Cantillo, Oscar.
Discovering Mission San Francisco de Asís / Oscar Cantillo.
pages cm. — (California missions)
Includes index.
ISBN 978-1-6271-3061-5 (hardcover) ISBN 978-1-5026-1209-0 (paperback) ISBN 978-1-6271-3063-9 (ebook)
1. San Francisco de Asís Mission (San Francisco, Calif.)—History—Juvenile literature. 2. Spanish mission buildings—California—San Francisco—History—Juvenile literature. 3. Franciscans—California—San Francisco—History—Juvenile literature. 4. Ohlone Indians—Missions—California—San Francisco—History—Juvenile literature. 5. California—History—To 1846—Juvenile literature. I. Title.

F869.S393C45 2015
979.4'61—dc23

2014003425

Editorial Director: Dean Miller
Editor: Kristen Susienka
Copy Editor: Cynthia Roby
Art Director: Jeffrey Talbot
Designer: Douglas Brooks
Photo Researcher: J8 Media
Production Manager: Jennifer Ryder-Talbot
Production Editor: David McNamara

The photographs in this book are used by permission and through the courtesy of: Cover photo by age fotostock/SuperStock; Mission San Francisco de Asis, founded June 1776 (photo), American School, (18th century)/San Francisco, California, USA/Photo © Barbara Singer/The Bridgeman Art Library, 1; Ambient Images Inc./SuperStock, 4; Courtesy of UC Berkeley, Bancroft Library, 8-9; Courtesy of UC Berkeley, Bancroft Library, 10; Courtesy CMRC, 12; © 2014 Pentacle Press, 14; Courtesy CMRC, 17; Tom Simondi/missiontour.org, 20-21; DEA/M. SEEMULLER/De Agostini Picture Library/Getty Images, 25; Courtesy CMRC, 26; Library of Congress Prints and Photographs Division, 28-29; Courtesy of UC Berkeley, Bancroft Library, 32; Courtesy CMRC, 33; John S Lander/LightRocket/Getty Images, 34; age fotostock/SuperStock, 41.

Printed in the United States of America

Contents

Mission San Francisco de Asís was the sixth of twenty-one missions in California.

1
The Spanish Explore Alta California

The heart of the city of San Francisco is home to a beautiful sandy building with two tall spires, each topped with a cross. This structure is Mission Dolores **Basilica**. Contrasting with the grand Basilica are the simple white walls and rust-colored tile roof of another smaller, older building that sits just beside: the original church of Mission San Francisco de Asís, usually called Mission Dolores. It is the sixth of twenty-one religious **settlements** called **missions** founded by Spanish colonists in California in the eighteenth and nineteenth centuries.

THE SPANISH ARRIVE IN THE NEW WORLD

The Spanish first became interested in California after Christopher Columbus discovered the lands that Europeans called the New World (North America, South America, and Central America) in 1492. At that time, Spain was a world power, eager to explore the New World in search of gold and other riches. The Spanish king, King Ferdinand, wanted to **claim** these lands and their resources for the Spanish empire. He also wanted to spread the

Catholic religion throughout the world. Catholicism is a **Christian** religion based on the teachings of Jesus Christ and the Bible. In addition to wanting to help the Roman Catholic Church with gold and other resources from the New World, the Spanish wanted to teach the many indigenous, or Native, people living in the New World about Christianity.

In 1542, Juan Rodríguez Cabrillo became one of the first Spanish explorers to reach the western coast of North America. He and his crew landed near San Diego—which Cabrillo named San Miguel—and claimed the land for their country.

At that time, the name *Las Californias*, meaning "the Californias," described both the area that is now the region of Mexico called the Baja Peninsula and the area that is the state of California. The Baja Peninsula was known as *Baja* (meaning "lower") California, while what is now the state of California was called *Alta* (meaning "upper") California.

When Cabrillo sailed to Alta California, he saw many Native people living along the coast. The Spanish crew traded cloth and trinkets with them for acorn bread and berries. In his journals, Cabrillo described the people he met as "friendly, generous, and peaceful."

The Spanish soon lost interest in this part of the world, however, since it did not have gold or other treasures like the lands of Central and South America had. It was almost 200 years later that Spain sent its first settlers to Alta California to set up military bases and to build missions.

2
The
Ohlone People

Before the arrival of the Spanish, indigenous Californians populated the land of Alta California in hundreds of small villages, divided by their own languages. Each village belonged to a different tribe, or group, and mostly the tribes lived in the same area. There were many groups from the Ohlone nation living near the San Francisco Bay area when the missionaries came in the late 1700s. Although the Native people identified themselves according to their village and not as a single group, the Spanish considered them as one, which they called *Coastaños,* meaning "coast people."

WHERE THE OHLONE CAME FROM

No one knows exactly when the first Ohlone people arrived in what is now California. Some think that many thousands of years ago people from Asia walked across the frozen land that once connected Siberia to Alaska. Slowly, they moved south, and over time populated the areas around San Francisco Bay.

HOW THE OHLONE GOT FOOD

The first Ohlone were hunters and gatherers, which meant they lived off the land, killing animals or collecting plants for their food.

The men used bows and arrows—the tips of which were made from sharp black stones called obsidian—to hunt game such as bear and deer. Because obsidian was not found in the area where the Ohlone lived, they traded nuts and clamshells to get the precious material from other tribes. They would also use baskets, made by the women of the tribe, to catch animals from the sea. The baskets were also used to gather food such as clams, onions, carrots, and grapes for the tribe to eat, to store food, to haul water, and to cook.

Acorns were especially important to the Ohlone's diet, since they were easy to find. When prepared correctly, they supplied

the people who ate them with **nutrients**. Each fall everyone would help to harvest them, and the women would grind the acorns into flour by using bowl-shaped rocks and stones. Acorns are poisonous, so the women had to wash the poison from the flour by pouring water over them many times. They were then able to use the flour to make bread, mush, and cake.

WHAT THE OHLONE WORE

The Ohlone also used items found in the area to make their clothing. During the warmer months, the men wore little or no clothing. The women wore grass skirts that tied together in the

The Ohlone who lived near San Francisco de Asís lived off the land around them, hunting and fishing using boats they built from wood and reeds.

Native people often decorated their bodies with paints made from minerals in the earth.

back. When the weather cooled, both men and women draped animal fur over their shoulders like a cape or robe. Sometimes they applied mud to their bodies to help keep them warm.

Both men and women wore their hair long, usually braided or in ponytails. Jewelry made from shells, leather, wood, bone, and feathers was also worn. Many Ohlone painted their faces for further decoration.

RELIGIOUS BELIEFS AND PRACTICES

According to their religion, the Ohlone respected people, the land, and all creatures of the earth. They believed that many spirits were at work in nature. The Ohlone believed other spirits brought sickness. They relied on *shamans* (healers) to cure the sick using herbs and other remedies. Also, because of their religious beliefs, the Ohlone considered some animals more **sacred** than others.

OTHER PASTIMES

Singing, dancing, and playing games were favorite pastimes of the Ohlone. They made their own musical instruments from gourds, wood, and bone. They were also very good at creating other objects such as boats and pipes from materials they had around them. Arts and crafts were a way for them to be creative and make useful tools.

When the Spanish came to build a mission in the area in the mid-1700s, the Ohlone way of life changed forever.

3
The
Mission System

The Spanish mission system was a way for the Spanish to populate a region and to ensure that the Native people living there were considered Spanish citizens. By becoming citizens of Spain, the Native people could not be claimed by other countries attempting to settle the area, such as Russia and Britain. The idea

© PENTACLE PRESS

The mission systems of Alta and Baja California were run by friars, who taught the Native people many skills, including farming and planting.

was to set up a mission in an area with a large indigenous population. Religious people, called **friars**, or *frays* in Spanish, would preach to the people, provide them a place to stay, teach them, and then **convert** them to their faith, called Christianity. Once the Native people accepted the Christian religion and Spanish lifestyle, they were called **neophytes** and considered subjects of Spain. They could not return to their tribes unless given permission, and later, many neophytes tried to leave.

There were Spanish missions already in place in other parts of the New World when the Spanish came to California. More than 200 years before the founding of Mission San Francisco de Asís, missionaries, soldiers, and settlers were sent to parts of North, Central, and South America to expand the Spanish empire. There they established a capital, which they named Mexico City, and called the surrounding lands **New Spain**. Today this land belongs to Mexico and the United States.

THE BEGINNING OF THE MISSIONS

The religious people involved in the missions were members of two Catholic orders, the Jesuits and the Franciscans. Both were devoted to helping the poor and sick, and spreading their faith. The Jesuits ran the missions of Baja California until 1767 when the Franciscans took over. The Franciscans then ran all of the missions until the 1820s.

To build the missions, missionaries, soldiers, and settlers worked together. Friars would encourage the Native people to stay and learn important skills, while the soldiers took possession of the land, guarding it by building *presidios*, or military fortresses. The few other settlers who came to California cleared the land for planting and began building *pueblos*, or towns, and ranches.

The Spanish government estimated that it would take ten years to train the Native people in Spanish work methods and religion. The mission lands would then be released back to the Native people for them to operate on their own. The land, however, would still belong to Spain and the Natives would be Spanish citizens. This process was called **secularization**.

The first missions of Baja California were thriving by the 1700s. The next place Spain set its sights on was north, in Alta California.

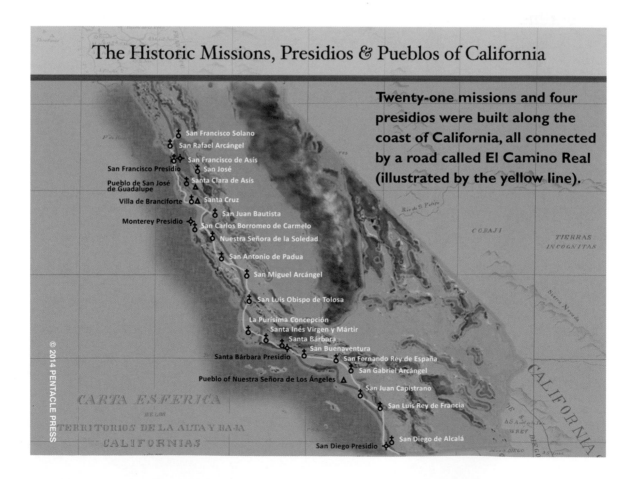

The Historic Missions, Presidios & Pueblos of California

Twenty-one missions and four presidios were built along the coast of California, all connected by a road called El Camino Real (illustrated by the yellow line).

San Francisco Solano
San Rafael Arcángel
San Francisco Presidio
San Francisco de Asís
San José
Pueblo de San José de Guadalupe
Santa Clara de Asís
Villa de Branciforte
Santa Cruz
Monterey Presidio
San Juan Bautista
San Carlos Borromeo de Carmelo
Nuestra Señora de la Soledad
San Antonio de Padua
San Miguel Arcángel
San Luis Obispo de Tolosa
La Purísima Concepción
Santa Inés Virgen y Mártir
Santa Bárbara
Santa Bárbara Presidio
San Buenaventura
San Fernando Rey de España
San Gabriel Arcángel
Pueblo of Nuestra Señora de Los Ángeles
San Juan Capistrano
San Luis Rey de Francia
San Diego Presidio
San Diego de Alcalá

© 2014 PENTACLE PRESS

4
The Founding of the Mission

The mission system in Alta California had twenty-one missions and was created over fifty-four years, between 1769 and 1823. The first mission, San Diego de Alcalá, started in 1769 and the others followed soon after. The structures were connected by a road called *El Camino Real,* which stretched across the coast and into Mexico. Three of the most important people involved in founding Mission San Francisco de Asís, which was established in 1776, were Fray Junípero Serra, Fray Francisco Palóu, and Fray Pedro Cambón.

FRAY SERRA

Fray Junípero Serra was born in Majorca, Spain, on November 24, 1713. He became a priest in 1737 and spent some years teaching philosophy. He knew that he wanted to spread his faith, so he later moved to New Spain and was put in charge of five missions in Baja California. When he was fifty-five years old, Serra was chosen by the Roman Catholic Church to head the Alta California missions, as their president. His first task was to found two missions in southern Alta California. He established one in San Diego and another in Monterey, more than 450 miles to the north. Although not present for the founding ceremony at Mission San Francisco de Asís, as mission president, Fray Serra was credited with the mission's founding. He died on August 28, 1784, at his headquarters, Mission San Carlos Borroméo del Río Carmelo, near Monterey.

FRAY PALÓU AND FRAY CAMBÓN

Fray Francisco Palóu and Fray Pedro Cambón were the first friars to take charge of Mission San Francisco de Asís. Born on January 22, 1723, in Spain, Fray Palóu became a friar in 1746. Like his former teacher, Fray Serra, Palóu became a **missionary** in New Spain. He arrived in 1773 at Mission San Diego de Alcalá. In 1774, he traveled with explorer and soldier Captain Fernando Rivera to select a site for the sixth mission. In June 1776, Palóu established Mission San Francisco de Asís, where he remained in charge until 1785.

Fray Cambón was a priest who arrived in Mexico in 1771. He knew a lot about agriculture, irrigation, and building construction, which made him important in establishing Mission San Francisco de Asís. He traveled with Fray Palóu in 1775 to the mission site and became cofounder upon their arrival in 1776.

FOUNDING MISSION SAN FRANCISCO DE ASÍS

The late 1700s saw many people flock to the Alta California region. Most were soldiers, sent to build fortresses to keep the Russians—who were also starting their own settlements in the northern part of the region—away. However, some were settlers and missionaries who built towns and religious communities to convert the Native people. Often the friars starting the missions were sent with an army to protect them against anyone who might try to attack them.

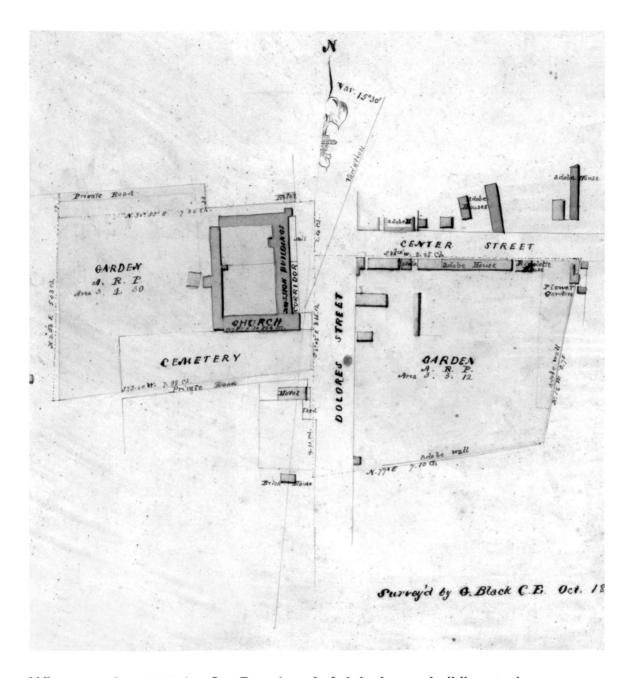

When completed, Mission San Francisco de Asís had many buildings on its property, as well as gardens, a cemetery, and lots of space for growing crops, as the layout here illustrates.

By 1774, the area where Mission San Francisco de Asís would sit had been located. However, Captain Rivera was afraid there wouldn't be enough soldiers to protect the land and the mission once it had been established, so he stalled the founding of the mission for two years. Captain Juan Bautista de Anza, an explorer who established many supply routes throughout Alta California including one near to Monterey, a few hundred miles from the mission site, brought help to the mission. In 1775, Anza led a caravan of 40 soldiers, 140 settlers (including women and children), 1,000 cattle, and 120 pack mules along his route, carrying supplies for Mission San Francisco de Asís. The travelers arrived at the presidio in Monterey on March 10, 1776. Once they had rested for a few months, another explorer, Lieutenant José Joaquín Maria Moraga, and founders Fray Palóu and Fray Cambón, led a group of about 180 settlers to the San Francisco area.

Mission San Francisco de Asís was founded on June 29, 1776, a few days before the Declaration of Independence was signed. However, it was not officially dedicated as a mission until October 9, 1776. The story of how the mission became also known as Mission Dolores arose during this time. Captain Anza had been exploring the area and came across a stream, which he called *Arroyo de los Dolores*, meaning "Creek of Sorrows." From then on, the mission was also known as Mission Dolores.

On the day of the founding in June 1776, Fray Palóu performed a Mass, or service, in celebration of the new mission. Lieutenant Moraga and the other soldiers with him then began building a temporary chapel to mark the sixth mission in Alta California.

5
Early Days

The mission in San Francisco took many years to build. During the first few years, the workers constructed many buildings from **adobe**. This included living quarters and offices for the missionaries, dormitories for the neophytes living at the mission, and a church. They also built a granary, a building in which grain is stored, and several kitchens. Many of these kitchens were called "*pozole* kitchens" and were used solely for making pozole, a stew made of vegetables, grain, and sometimes meat. These times signaled new changes to the area, which affected not only the land but also the people: the settlers, soldiers, and especially the Native population that lived there.

CONSTRUCTING THE MISSION

Soon after construction on the chapel began in 1776, the soldiers and settlers from New Spain started building the presidio overlooking the bay. This was a large fortress where the soldiers would live, and it would be used to look for any threat, such as armies and even Native people who were unhappy because the Spaniards were building on the land.

Once the construction was well under way, several of the workers began to build more permanent structures on the site of the mission, such as priests' quarters and living areas for the Native people whom they hoped to convert. These were completed over the next few years.

As the friars and soldiers began to build, some of the Ohlone ventured to the site. They were curious to see what the newcomers were doing, and were drawn by the Spanish trinkets and tools, most of which were unlike anything they had ever seen before. The friars were delighted because this was an opportunity to try to convert the Native people. They preached to the Ohlone, convincing some that they were creating a sort of utopia by bringing this mission and the Kingdom of God to the area. Some Native people believed them and moved into the mission. But many other Ohlone were skeptical—how could they trust these new people?

FOUNDING CELEBRATION

The official dedication of the mission was held on October 9, 1776, just days after the religious holiday, or **feast day**, honoring Saint Francis of Assisi, for whom the mission was named. During the

ceremony, the participants erected a cross at the mission site. Then they sang, rang bells, and fired off muskets and cannons.

The blasts of the cannons and muskets fired during the founding ceremonies scared off the Ohlone, who were unfamiliar with such weapons. When the Ohlone eventually returned to see what the Spanish were doing, again they appreciated the gifts the missionaries and settlers offered them, but not all trusted the strangers.

COMMUNITY GROWS

As the mission buildings started to be created, more Native people arrived at the mission and watched as the Spanish used tools made of metal to cut down trees and make building supports. Some of the Ohlone wanted to try these tools and offered to help. The Spanish agreed, as they needed the Ohlone people to help them build. They also knew that working together to build the mission buildings was a good opportunity to introduce the Ohlone to Spanish work methods.

This model of Mission San Francisco de Asís shows what the grounds would have looked like in the 1800s.

The Spanish and the Ohlone gathered the materials they needed to make the structures. Since the area was rich in forests of redwood and other trees, the builders chopped many of them into planks for the buildings, then used *carretas*—small wooden carts pulled by oxen or mules—to move the lumber to the mission site.

Bricks for the walls were made from adobe, a mixture of clay, water, straw, and sometimes manure. The missionaries showed the Ohlone men, women, and children how to mix the ingredients together by crushing them with their feet or by having animals stomp on them. They poured the mixture into wooden molds to make rectangular bricks, and then let the bricks dry in the sun until they hardened. After, they built walls, using mud to hold the bricks in place.

In return for helping the friars, the Ohlone showed the missionaries and settlers how to make buildings using reeds and twigs bundled together and plastered with clay to keep the rain out. For defense, the Spanish also built fences called *palizadas*.

COMPLETING THE MISSION

As the construction continued, stables, carpentry shops, workrooms, and a new church were added to the complex. Farmers planted crops and orchards in the soil surrounding the mission. As they built, the friars preached and more of the Ohlone converted to Christianity. However, at first the mission didn't have a large neophyte population. In 1783, there were only 215 living there. Nonetheless, the mission's grounds continued to grow, and even though its location moved about half a mile from the original site in 1781, by 1798, San Francisco de Asís was completed.

6
Daily Life at the Mission

As at the other missions, the missionaries and soldiers at Mission San Francisco de Asís established a strict daily schedule for the neophytes who lived there.

DAILY SCHEDULE

As the sun began to rise, the mission residents woke to the sound of bells ringing in the *campanario* (bell tower). They were then brought together to attend church for Mass, morning prayers, and church lessons. These religious duties were followed by breakfast. For a time, the neophytes at Mission San Francisco de Asís were only given dry grain to eat, while neophytes at most missions were fed *atole*, a porridge made of corn or grain.

After breakfast, it was time for work. Jobs were assigned to both men and women. In addition to cooking, the Ohlone women made baskets, soap, and cloth. The Spanish brought European looms so they could teach the women to weave fabric. The women used the fabric to make clothes for the men, children, soldiers, and themselves. They also made wool blankets to keep people warm at night.

The Spanish taught the Ohlone men how to farm, raise livestock, and create goods for trade. Among the skills they learned were tanning, leatherworking, carpentry, blacksmithing, and construction. The missionaries often brought in craftsmen from missions in New Spain to teach these trades. During the day, some of the friars worked alongside the neophytes.

At Mission San Francisco de Asís, the Ohlone raised livestock, including cattle, sheep, mules, and horses. They planted wheat, corn, beans, barley, peas, lentils, and fruit trees. Eventually, the Ohlone women began to use corn and wheat flour rather than acorn flour. When time permitted, they still gathered nuts and edible plants, especially in the early years of the mission.

The workers took a break for lunch. Eventually, meals of dry grain were replaced by *pozole*. After lunch they took a rest or nap, called a *siesta*. Then work resumed in the afternoon.

Another Mass was held before supper. The evening concluded with more prayers, church instruction, Spanish-language lessons, and some time to relax. The Native people enjoyed singing, dancing, and playing games during their free time.

Fiestas, or festivals, were sometimes held. These events broke up the routine of mission life. The Catholics held fiestas in honor of various saints, weddings, births, and important events in church history. The Ohlone were able to observe some of their traditional ceremonies, too. The friars believed that such rituals were against Catholic teachings but allowed the Ohlone rituals to take place because they wanted to maintain peaceful relationships at the mission. On one occasion, the friars even asked the Ohlone to perform a traditional Ohlone dance to impress a Russian expedition that came to the mission in 1816.

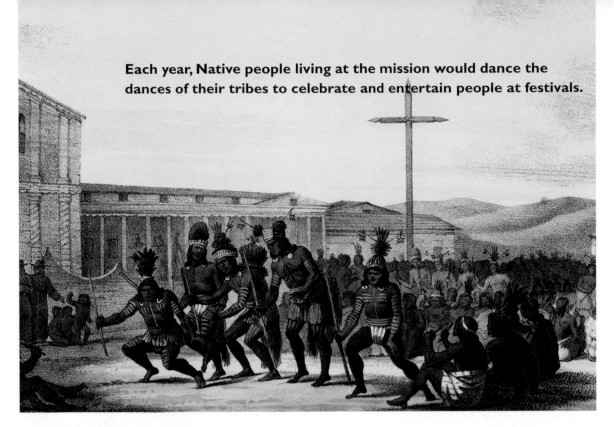

Each year, Native people living at the mission would dance the dances of their tribes to celebrate and entertain people at festivals.

A DIFFICULT LIFE

Life presented challenges for everyone at the mission. The Ohlone were often frustrated and angry at being kept on the mission grounds, sometimes against their will. Also, the Ohlone were not the only Native tribes brought to Mission San Francisco de Asís. Native people from other tribes such as the Miwok and Patwin also lived there. Many felt that they had been unfairly brought into mission life and did not want to become Catholic, follow the friars' rules, or be subjected to the abusive treatment of the Spanish soldiers.

The Spanish friars and soldiers often felt isolated being so far away from their friends, family, and homeland. They were not used to Alta California's climate, environment, and way of life. They didn't have many of the comforts they had known in Spain and New Spain. Living quarters were rustic and included only a simple wooden cot with a single, coarse blanket. The food was often bland.

The friars at all the missions taught neophytes Spanish work methods and religious beliefs.

A MISSIONARY'S LIFE

The life of a missionary was filled with many tasks. In addition to their religious lessons, missionaries taught the Ohlone about Spanish trades and farming and ranching techniques. They were responsible for performing religious services, such as Mass, funerals, weddings, and baptisms. The missionaries also had to manage the soldiers, who were often rough.

The friars were responsible for keeping detailed records about population and production at the mission, which were communicated to the government in New Spain. Historians have learned a lot about life at Mission San Francisco de Asís from these records. For example, these records show that 1,242 neophytes lived there in 1820. In 1832, the mission owned 3,500 sheep, 5,000 cattle, 1,000 horses, and 18 mules. The friars also noted a total of 2,043 marriages, 5,166 deaths, and 6,898 baptisms in a sixty-year period. From 1785 to 1832, the workers harvested more than 70,000 bushels of barley, 18,000 bushels of corn, and 120,000 bushels of wheat.

7
The Decline of the Mission

As time went on, the neophytes grew frustrated and resentful of the mission system. Tensions between the Spanish and Ohlone at Mission San Francisco de Asís grew, making it difficult for everyone living and working there.

PROBLEMS ARISE

Besides the fact that all neophytes were forbidden to leave the mission unless granted permission and would be severely punished if they tried, daily life was strict and labor-intensive. Many Native people living at San Francisco de Asís had become restless and unhappy.

Also, single neophyte girls and women were required to live separately from the other residents. They lived in dormitories, called *monjeríos*, which were locked at night to keep the girls in and others out. This meant that families who were at the mission together were separated. The mission doors were also locked at night to prevent people from leaving or thieves from sneaking in. Still, many tried to escape. They often hid out in the Contra Costa, the opposite side of the bay. Those who escaped and were caught were rounded up and returned to the mission, where they were punished, usually by being whipped or beaten.

Yet many Ohlone and other Native tribes there managed to get away from Mission San Francisco de Asís. In 1795 approximately 280 neophytes ran away, followed by more than 200 over the next year. Some of those who escaped wanted to join tribes outside of the mission, where they could live a traditional lifestyle. Others wanted go to other settlements in the area and try to live free lives there. After a time, the soldiers grew tired of hunting down runaways. This frustrated the missionaries because they wanted the indigenous people brought back to the mission. As a result, sometimes other neophytes, who were loyal to the mission, were sent to search for runaways. In one search in the 1790s, about seven

Life at the mission was not easy, and many Native people tried to escape.

neophytes who had escaped were killed outside of the mission complex by other neophytes of Mission San Francisco de Asís.

ILLNESS HITS THE MISSION

The San Francisco climate was often cool and damp. As a result, much of the soil in the area was poor for growing crops, and the neophytes and missionaries often didn't have enough food.

The climate also contributed to sickness and disease at Mission San Francisco de Asís. Many of the Native people found themselves becoming sick with diseases common in Spain but unknown in Alta California. Their bodies had not built up any resistance to diseases such as measles and smallpox, and many

died as a result. In March 1806, the mission was hit with a measles outbreak that resulted in 471 deaths, a devastating loss to the neophyte population there.

Those who survived the epidemic had trouble recovering in the San Francisco climate. They also had trouble because of the living conditions at the mission. Many of the living quarters were cramped, especially the *monjeríos*, and the adobe buildings were damp inside. This caused the residents to develop breathing problems. Additionally, the mission's poor sanitation systems attracted bugs and rodents. In 1816, Otto Von Kotzebue, a Russian explorer who had visited the mission, wrote, "The uncleanliness in these barracks baffles description, and this is perhaps the cause of the great mortality." While on an expedition to the area in the 1820s, the explorer Frederick William Beechey wrote about the neophyte homes: "Their hovels afforded scarcely any protection against the weather, and were black with smoke: Some of the Indians were sleeping on the greasy floor."

Many neophytes at Mission San Francisco de Asís succumbed to disease and died. Those who remained began to doubt their new Christian faith. In order to help those neophytes who were suffering from illness, the friars sent the sick to San Rafael to the north side of San Francisco Bay in 1817. San Rafael was a branch mission, or *asistencia*, a smaller religious community set up by the members of another mission. A friar who had studied medicine, named Luís Gil y Taboada, was placed in charge of the asistencia. More than 300 people were sent to San Rafael. There, many sick were able to recover in the warm sunshine.

8
Secularization

In 1810, the Mexican War of Independence began. Residents of New Spain fought for eleven years to break off from the Spanish government in Europe. During this time, the Spanish government required the people living at the missions to work harder to provide food and clothing to the Spanish soldiers. After New Spain gained independence in 1821, the people formed a new nation called Mexico, which now had authority over the missions in Alta California.

THE SPANISH MISSIONS UNDER MEXICAN RULE

The Mexican government was not happy with the state of the missions. Some officials thought that the neophytes were being treated as slaves. Others saw the richness of the mission lands and wanted to take them so they could become wealthy. In August 1833, the Mexican government finally decided to secularize the missions. However, the secularization process did not occur as the Spanish had planned. Rather than turning the mission land and property over to the Native people, the Mexican government's Secularization Act of 1833 took control of the mission property away from the Catholic Chruch and gave it to the government.

A small portion of the mission lands, buildings, livestock, and crops were distributed to the Native people. Much of the area was

Even after secularization, the mission celebrated Saint Francis of Assisi's feast day with bullfights and festivals.

taken over by local landowners, who either took the land outright, bought land from corrupt Mexican officials, or were given land as gifts from Mexican authorities. Under Mexican law, it was acceptable for the new owners of mission lands to keep the neophytes on as slaves.

SECULARIZING SAN FRANCISCO DE ASÍS

Mission San Francisco de Asís was secularized in 1834. Most of the Ohlone and other tribes living there at that time left the mission and moved into San Francisco (which was now a city) or to nearby towns, taking jobs as servants, laborers, cooks, or *vaqueros* (cowboys). Some tried to return to their former life, but most of their villages had been taken over by missions or settlers.

THE END OF ALTA CALIFORNIA

Mexico did not rule California for long. In the 1840s, American settlers flocked to California in search of gold. The new settlers petitioned the United States government to make California a state. A war between the U.S. and Mexico for control of Alta California broke out in 1846. In 1848, the fighting ended with Mexico giving up the region. Alta California became a state and was renamed California in 1850. In the late 1850s, United Sates president James Buchanan returned portions of the mission lands in San Francisco to the Roman Catholic Church.

This drawing by Oriana Day shows Mission Dolores around the time it was secularized.

Today Mission San Francisco de Asís is a historical site with two churches, gardens, a cemetery, and a museum.

9
Mission San Francisco de Asís Today

The nineteenth century saw the city of San Francisco grow rapidly. At this time, parts of Mission San Francisco de Asís were converted into businesses such as a boarding house, a print shop, and several saloons. By 1876, the population of San Francisco had grown so large that the little chapel could no longer serve the city. On the 100-year anniversary of the founding of Mission San Francisco de Asís, a much larger church was opened next to the original chapel. However, in 1906, an earthquake reduced this new church to rubble, while the little chapel remained standing.

THE CHAPEL

The original chapel is the oldest building in San Francisco today. It is 114 feet long and 22 feet wide. Inside, the chapel is decorated with Ohlone and Catholic designs and murals. Many of the designs on the walls and support beams were first painted on canvas and then plastered to the walls. The *reredos* (a large backboard and table used in religious services) covers most of the far wall.

A cemetery is located just south of the chapel. In it are the graves of some of California's first settlers and more than 5,000 Native people who lived at the mission.

THE CHURCHES

After the earthquake in 1906, the Catholics began building another, even larger, house of worship. This church, currently called Mission Dolores Basilica, was completed in 1918. In 1952, Pope Pius XII, the head of the Roman Catholic Church at that time, officially designated the church as a basilica. It continues to serve the surrounding community as a parish church.

Today, Mission San Francisco de Asís is both a tourist attraction and a functioning part of the San Francisco community. In addition to the two churches, the mission contains a museum and gift shop.

The two churches of Mission San Francisco de Asís stand side by side on Dolores Street in the Mission District of San Francisco. Along the corridor walls leading from one church to the other are sketches and photographs made during different periods of the mission's history. Visitors from around the world come to the mission to catch a glimpse of how the early Californians lived.

The California missions are an integral part of the state's history. Each represents a complicated story about how the state came to be. While a great conquest for the Spanish, the missions were also the source of much pain and suffering for California's indigenous population. Like the other missions, Mission San Francisco de Asís is a key part of that historical legacy.

10
Make Your Own Mission Model

To make your own model of Mission San Francisco de Asís, you will need:

- cardboard
- dry lasagna noodles
- felt (red)
- glue
- glue gun (optional)
- paint (black and white)

- pins
- Popsicle sticks
- skill sticks
- Styrofoam
- toothpicks
- yarn (red)

DIRECTIONS

Adult supervision is suggested.

Step 1: Cut out a piece of Styrofoam measuring 21" × 10" (53.34 cm × 25.4 cm) for the base.

21"

10"

Step 2: To make the first floor of the church, cut four pieces of Styrofoam 12" × 6.5" (30.48 cm × 16.51 cm). Stick the walls together with pins.

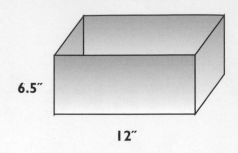

Step 3: Cut out two Styrofoam walls measuring 5" × 6.5" (12.7 cm × 16.51 cm). Pin them on the left side of the structure.

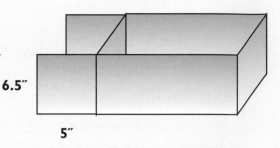

Step 4: To make the second story of the church, cut two pieces of cardboard measuring 11" × 7" (27.94 cm × 17.78 cm). Cut the top corners off to form a triangle. The walls should be 4" (10.16 cm) high.

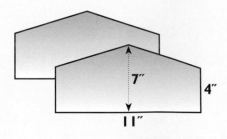

Step 5: Cut out two cardboard sidewalls measuring 11" × 4" (27.94 cm × 10.16 cm). Paint all the pieces of the church's second story white.

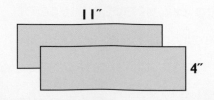

Step 6: Glue the front, side, and back walls together. Attach the second floor to the Styrofoam first floor of the church.

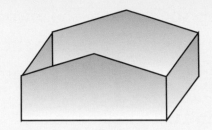

Step 7: To make the roof, cut a piece of cardboard measuring 20″ × 12″ (50.8 cm × 30.48 cm). Bend it in half and glue it in place. Cover the roof with red felt.

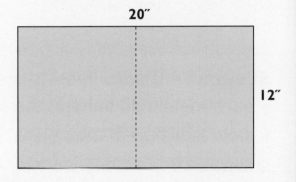

Step 8: For the roof to cover the two small side walls, cut out a piece of cardboard measuring 12″ × 6″ (30.48 cm × 14.24 cm). Glue the lasagna noodles on top. Allow the noodles to dry and then paint them red.

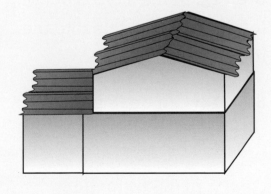

Step 9: Make the balcony by gluing Popsicle sticks and toothpicks to the front of the top floor (see page 40).

Step 10: To make the lower columns, glue Popsicle sticks to the first floor of the church.

Step 11: To make the top columns, glue sugar cubes to the second story above the balcony.

Step 12: To make windows, cut a Popsicle stick into three pieces. Paint each piece black, and glue onto the top story of the church.

Step 13: Make a cross out of toothpicks and glue it to the roof.

Step 14: Cut out a piece of cardboard to make the doors. Paint it and allow it to dry. Glue it to the front of the bottom of the church.

Step 15: To decorate the mission grounds, glue on miniature fake trees, bushes, and flowers.

The model of Mission
San Francisco de Asís.

Key Dates in Mission History

1492   Christopher Columbus reaches the West Indies

1542   Cabrillo's expedition to California

1602   Sebastián Vizcaíno sails to California

1713   Fray Junípero Serra is born

1769   Founding of San Diego de Alcalá

1770   Founding of San Carlos Borroméo del Río Carmelo

1771   Founding of San Antonio de Padua and San Gabriel Arcángel

1772   Founding of San Luis Obispo de Tolosa

1775–76   Founding of San Juan Capistrano

1776   Founding of San Francisco de Asís

1776   Declaration of Independence is signed

1777	Founding of Santa Clara de Asís
1782	Founding of San Buenaventura
1784	Fray Serra dies
1786	Founding of Santa Bárbara
1787	Founding of La Purísima Concepción
1791	Founding of Santa Cruz and Nuestra Señora de la Soledad
1797	Founding of San José, San Juan Bautista, San Miguel Arcángel, and San Fernando Rey de España
1798	Founding of San Luis Rey de Francia
1804	Founding of Santa Inés
1817	Founding of San Rafael Arcángel
1823	Founding of San Francisco Solano
1833	Mexico passes Secularization Act
1848	Gold found in northern California
1850	California becomes the thirty-first state

Glossary

adobe (uh-DOH-bee) Sun-dried bricks made of straw, mud, and sometimes manure.

basilica (bah-SILL-ih-kuh) A large Catholic church with an aisle that leads to a tall, curved wall. Special ceremonies such as ordinations to the priesthood are held in the basilica.

Christian (KRIS-chin) Someone who follows the teachings of Jesus Christ and the Bible.

claim (KLAYM) When people take something that they say belongs to them, they "lay a claim" on it.

convert (kun-VURT) To change religious beliefs.

feast day (FEEST DAY) A day in the Catholic religious group that celebrates a particular saint.

friar (FRY-ur) A brother in a communal religious order. Friars can also be priests.

mission (MISH-in) A religious community set up by an order of the Catholic church to introduce Christianity to Native people of an area.

missionary (MIH-shuh-nayr-ee) A person who teaches his or her religion to people with different beliefs.

neophyte (NEE-oh-fyt) Name for Native Americans who were baptized into the Christian faith.

New Spain (NOO SPAYN) The area in North America where the Spanish colonists established their capital; New Spain later became Mexico.

nutrients (NOO-tree-ints)
Substances that supply energy
to plants, animals, and humans.
Nutrients are needed to live
and to grow.

sacred (SAY-kred) Highly
respected and considered
very important.

secularization (sehk-yoo-luh-rih-ZAY-shun) A process by
which the mission lands were
made to be nonreligious.

settlement (SEH-tul-ment)
A small village or group of
houses.

Pronunciation Guide

asistencias (a-sis-TEN-see-uhs)

atole (ah-TOH-lay)

campanario (kahm-pah-NAR-ee-oh)

carreta (kah-REH-tah)

fray (FRAY)

monjerío (mon-hay-REE-oh)

palizada (pa-lee-ZAH-da)

pozole (po-ZOH-lay)

siesta (see-EHS-tah)

vaqueros (bah-KEHR-ohs)

Find Out More

To learn more about the California missions and Mission San Francisco de Asís, check out these books and websites.

BOOKS

Bibby, Brian. *The Fine Art of California Indian Basketry*. Berkeley, CA: Heydey, 2013.

Richards, Rand. *Historic San Francisco: A Concise History and Guide*. San Francisco, CA: Heritage House Publishers, 2007.

Weber, Francis J. *Blessed Fray Junípero Serra: An Outstanding California Hero*. Bowling Green, MO: Editions Du Signe, 2008.

White, Tekla. *San Francisco Bay Area Missions*. Minneapolis, MN: Lerner Publishing, 2008.

Williams, Jack S. *The Ohlone of California*. New York, NY: Rosen Publishing Group, 2003.

WEBSITES

California Mission Internet Trail

www.escusd.k12.ca.us/mission_trail/MissionTrail.html
Explore all California missions via virtual field trips. View photos, student art, and maps. Resources for teachers are also available on this website.

California Missions Resource Center

www.missionscalifornia.com
Interact with a mission timeline, videos, and photo gallery and unlock key facts about each mission in the California mission system.

Encyclopedia of San Francisco

www.sfhistoryencyclopedia.com
Visit this growing web-based project of the San Francisco Museum and Historical Society and discover the rich history of the city of San Francisco.

Mission San Francisco de Asís (Mission Dolores) Website

www.missiondolores.org
Visit the official website of Mission San Francisco de Asís to discover facts about the mission's history and how it operates today.

Index